Wolfgang Amadeus Mozart
(1756–1791)

Klavierstücke
Piano Pieces
Morceaux pour piano

Urtext

Herausgegeben von · Edited by · Edité par
István Máriássy
K 113
Könemann Music Budapest

INDEX

Nannerls Notenbuch · Nannerl's Notebook · Petit livre de musique de Nannerl

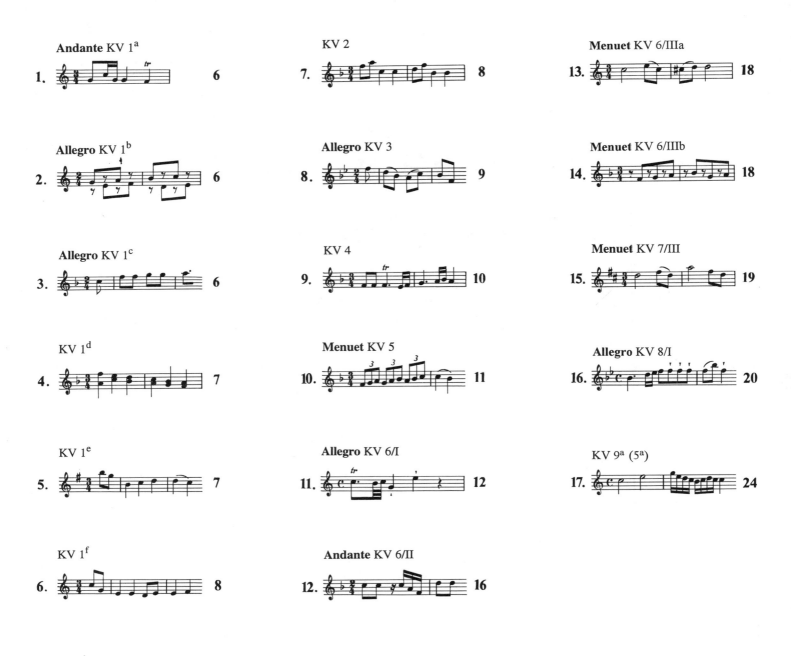

Londoner Skizzenbuch · The London Sketchbook · Carnet d'esquisses de Londres

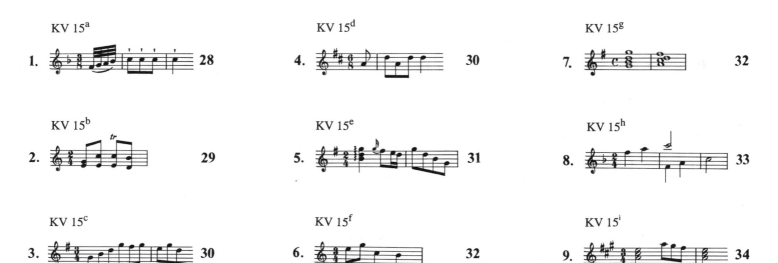

KV 15^{k}

10.  34

KV 15^{l}

11.  35

KV 15^{m}

12.  36

KV 15^{n}

13.  36

KV 15°

14.  38

KV 15^{p}

15.  40

KV 15^{q}

16.  44

KV 15^{r}

17.  45

KV 15^{s}

18.  47

KV 15^{t}

19.  47

KV 15^{u}

20.  52

KV 15^{v}

21.  53

KV 15^{w}

22.  56

KV 15^{x}

23.  58

KV 15^{y}

24.  60

KV 15^{z}

25.  60

KV 15^{aa}

26.  62

KV 15^{bb}

27.  64

KV 15^{cc}

28.  66

KV 15^{dd}

29.  68

KV 15^{ee}

30. 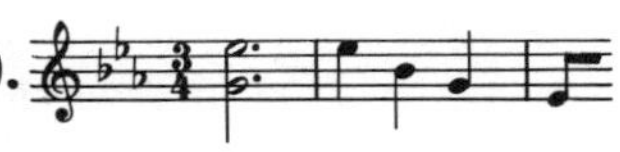 70

KV 15^{ff}

31.  70

KV 15^{gg}

32.  71

KV 15^{hh}

33. 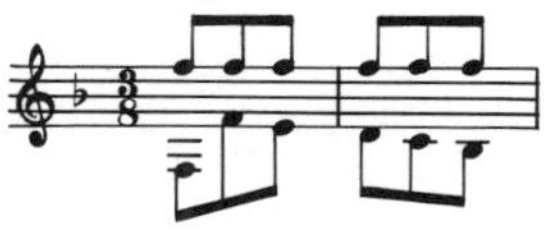 72

KV 15^{ii}

34.  74

KV 15^{kk}

35.  76

Presto KV 15^{ll}

36.  78

KV 15^{mm}

37.  79

KV 15^{oo}

38.  79

KV 15^{pp}

39.  80

KV 15^{qq}

40.  80

Einzelstücke · Separate Pieces · Pièces separés

Klavierstück in F KV 33B

83

Modulierendes Präludium KV deest

84

Präludium (Capriccio) in C KV 395 (300^g)
Allegretto

86

Ouverture (Suite) KV 399 (385^i)
Grave

92

Marche funebre KV 453^a
Lento

102

Adagio in h KV 540
Adagio

103

Gigue in G KV 574
Allegro

108

Menuetto in D KV 355 (576^b)

110

Fingerübungen KV 626^b/48

114

Tänze und Marsch · Dances and March · Danses et marche

12 Menuette KV 103 (61^d)

118

Menuett in C KV 61^g/II

130

Menuett in D KV 94(73^h)

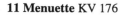

131

11 Menuette KV 176

132

Kontretänze KV 269^b
Allegro

142

8 Menuette KV 315^a(315^g)

146

Marcia KV 408/1(383^e)
Maestoso

154

6 Tedeschi KV 509

158

Nannerls Notenbuch

Des Wolfgangerl Compositiones in den ersten 3 Monaten nach seinem 5ten Jahre.

Andante

KV 1^a

1.

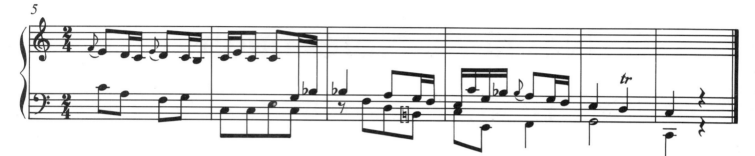

Allegro

KV 1^b

2.

Sgr: Wolfgango Mozart 11ten Decembris 1761

Allegro

KV 1^c

3.

K 113

Menuetto del Sgr. Wolfgango Mozart 16to Decembris 1761

KV 1^d

KV 1^e
Salzburg, ca 1761–64

6.

7.

KV 3
del Sgr: Wolfgango Mozart 1762. d. 4ten Martij

8.

K 113

9

9.

Menuet

KV 5
Salzburg, 1762

10.

Allegro

11.

12.

Menuet

KV 6/IIIa
Bruxelles, 1763

Menuet I

13.

KV 6/IIIb
di Wolfgango Mozart d. 16ten July 1762

Menuet II

14.

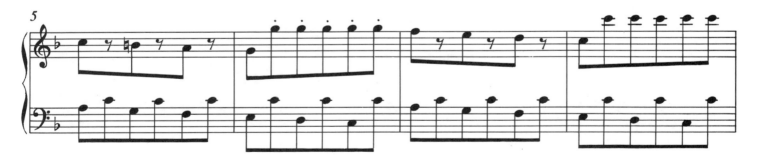

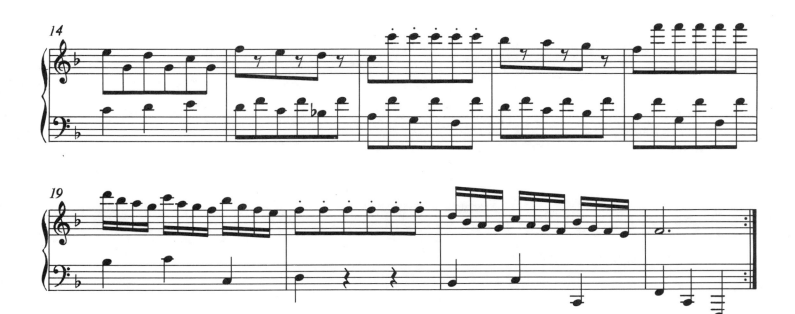

Menuet I da capo

Menuet

KV 7/III
di Wolfgango Mozart d. 30ᵗᵉⁿ Novbr: 1763 à Paris

15.

Allegro

16.

22

KV 9ª /5ª/
ca 1764

17.

26

Londoner Skizzenbuch

1.

2.

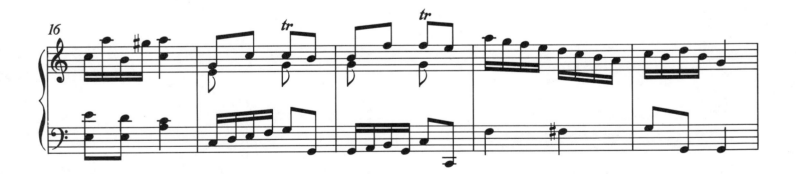

3.

4.

Da capo

KV 15ᵉ

5.

6.

7.

KV 15^h

8.

Da capo

9.

10.

11.

[Da capo]

12.

13.

14.

15.

42

16.

KV 15ʳ

17.

18.

Da capo

19.

48

20.

21.

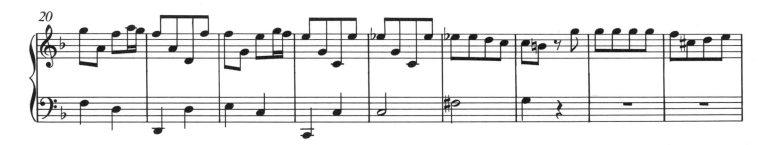

22.

23.

24.

25.

38

44

50

56

KV 15ᵃᵃ

26.

27.

28.

29.

30.

31.

32.

Da capo

Da capo

Da capo

33.

Fine

Da capo

34.

K 113

35.

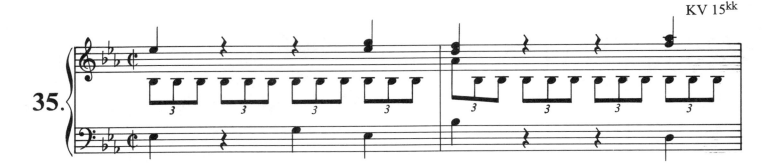

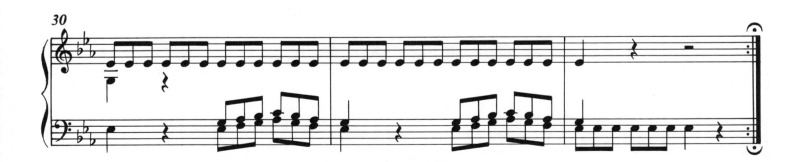

Presto

36.

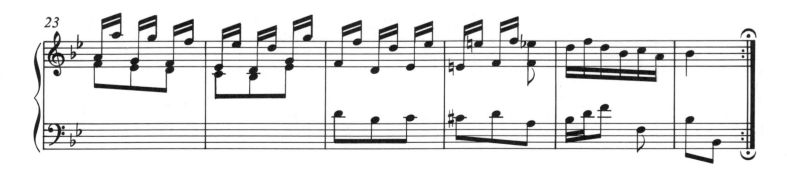

37.

[Da capo]

38.

39.

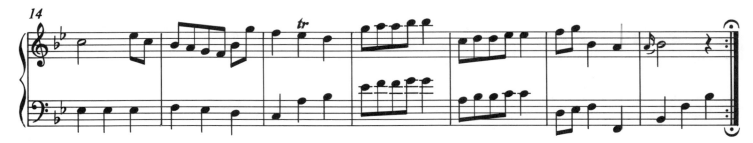

40.

Einzelstücke

Klavierstück in F

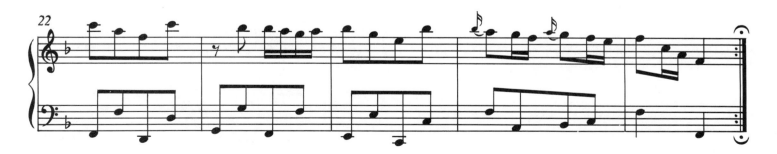

K 113

83

Modulierendes Präludium

KV deest
Salzburg, 1766–67

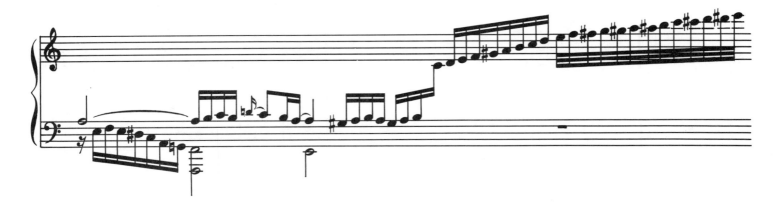

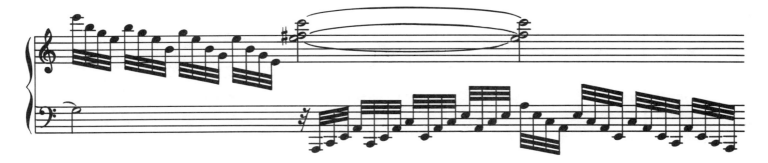

K 113

Präludium (Capriccio) in C

KV 395 (300^g)
München, 1777

Allegretto

Capriccio

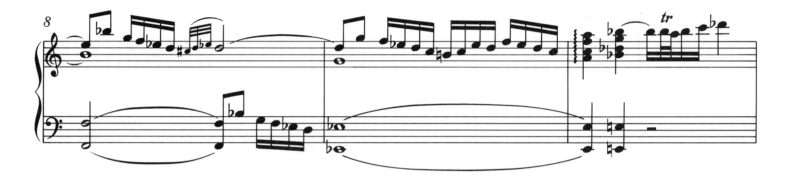

88

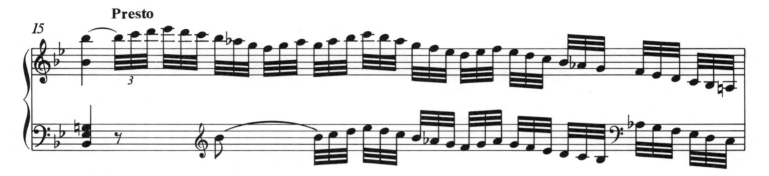

Capriccio

Allegro assai

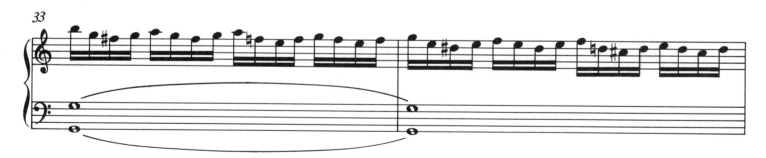

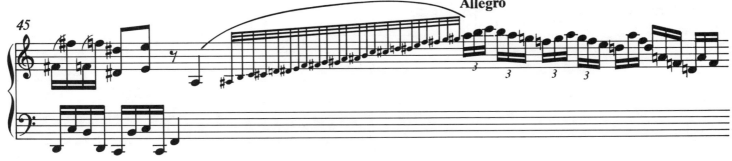

Ouverture (dans le Style de G. F. Händel)

KV 399 (385ⁱ)
Wien, ca 1782

Grave

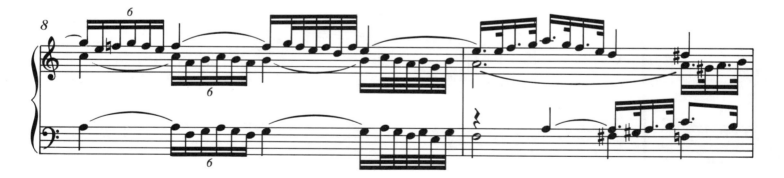

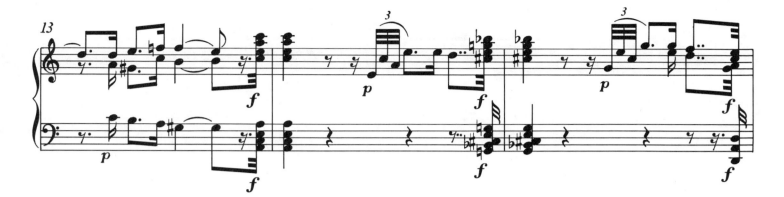

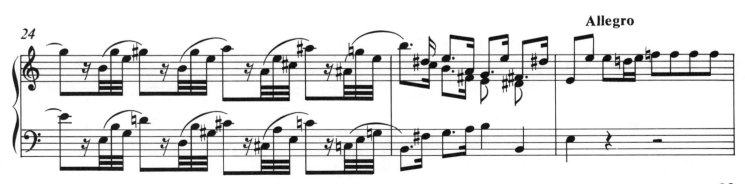

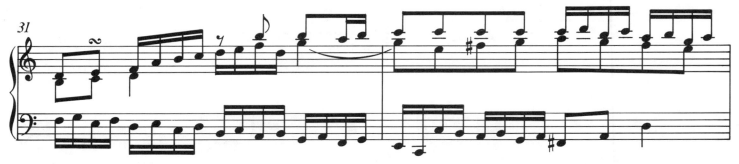

94

Allemande

Andante

98

Courante

Allegretto

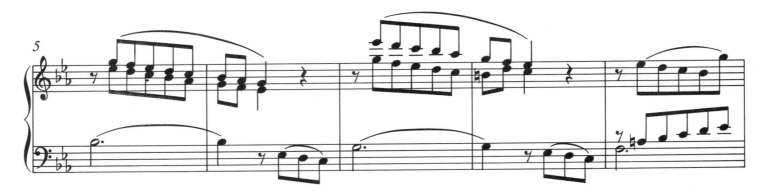

Marche funebre

KV 453ᵃ
del Sigr. Maestro Contrapunto
Wien, 1784

Adagio in h

Adagio

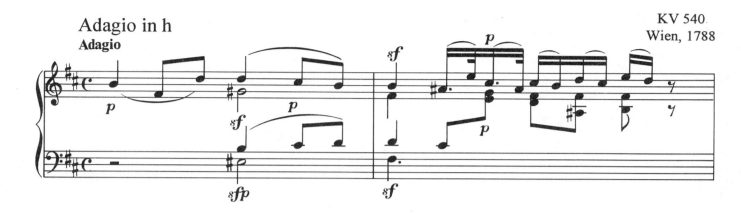

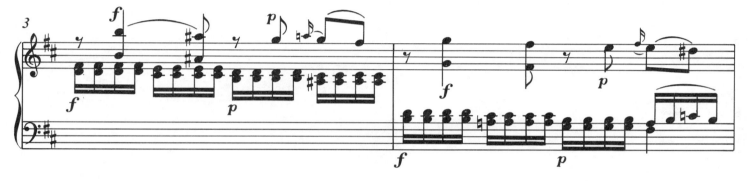

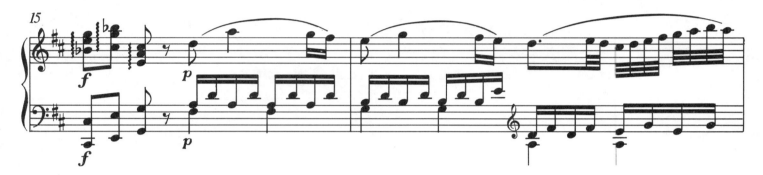

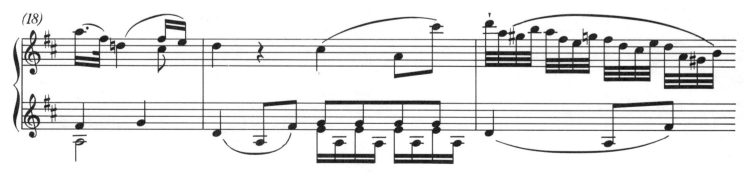

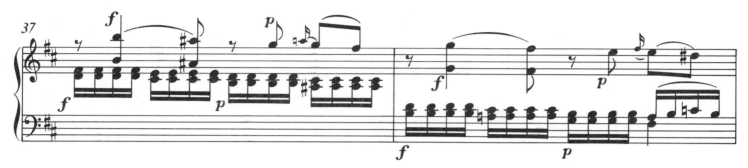

106

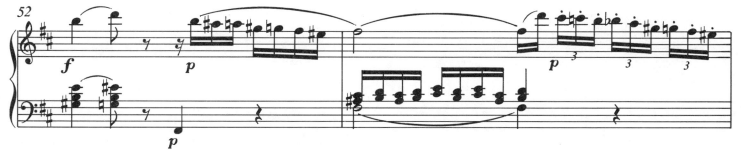

Gigue in G

KV 574
Leipzig, 1789

Allegro

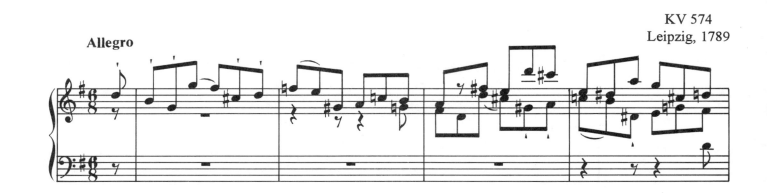

Menuetto in D

KV 355 (576^b)
Wien, ca 1789–90

Menuetto da W.A. Mozart

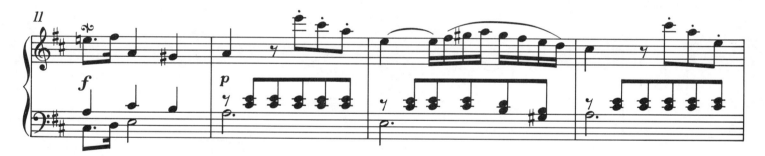

mancando

dolce

Segue Trio

Trio da M. Stadler

112

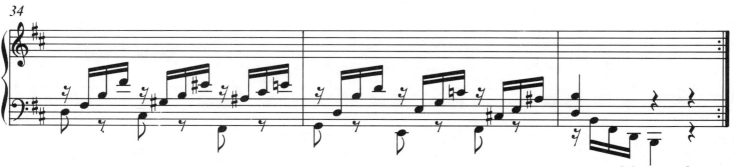

Menuetto da capo

Fingerübungen

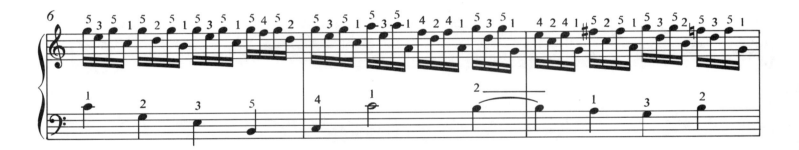

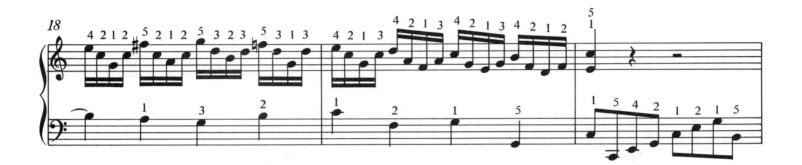

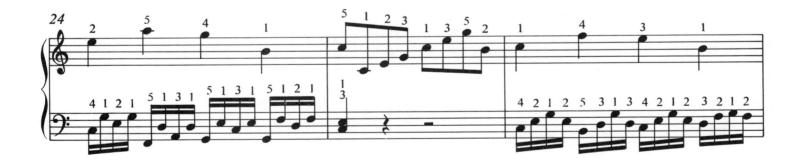

[repet. senza fine]

Tänze und Marsch

12 Menuette

KV 103 (61^d)
Salzburg, ca 1772

1.

Trio

Menuetto da capo

2.

Trio

Menuetto da capo

3.

Trio

Menuetto da capo

4.

Trio

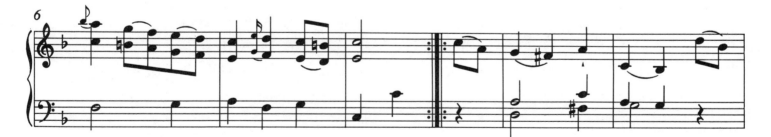

Menuetto da capo

5.

Trio

Menuetto da capo

6.

Trio

Menuetto da capo

7.

Trio

Menuetto da capo

8.

Trio

Menuetto da capo

9.

Trio

Menuetto da capo

10.

Trio

Menuetto da capo

11.

Trio

Menuetto da capo

12.

Trio

Menuetto da capo

Menuett in C

KV 61^g/II
1770

Menuet

Trio

Menuetto da capo

K 113

Menuett in D

ll Menuette

KV 176
Salzburg, 1773

1.

Trio

Menuetto da capo

K 113

2.

Trio

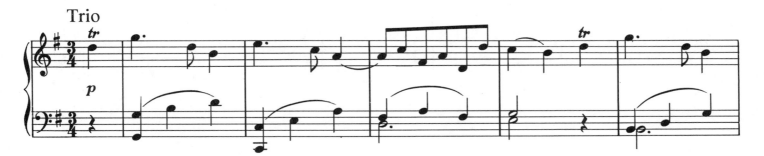

Menuetto da capo

134

5.

Trio

Menuetto da capo

6.

Trio

7.

Trio

Menuetto da capo

8.

Trio

Menuetto da capo

9.

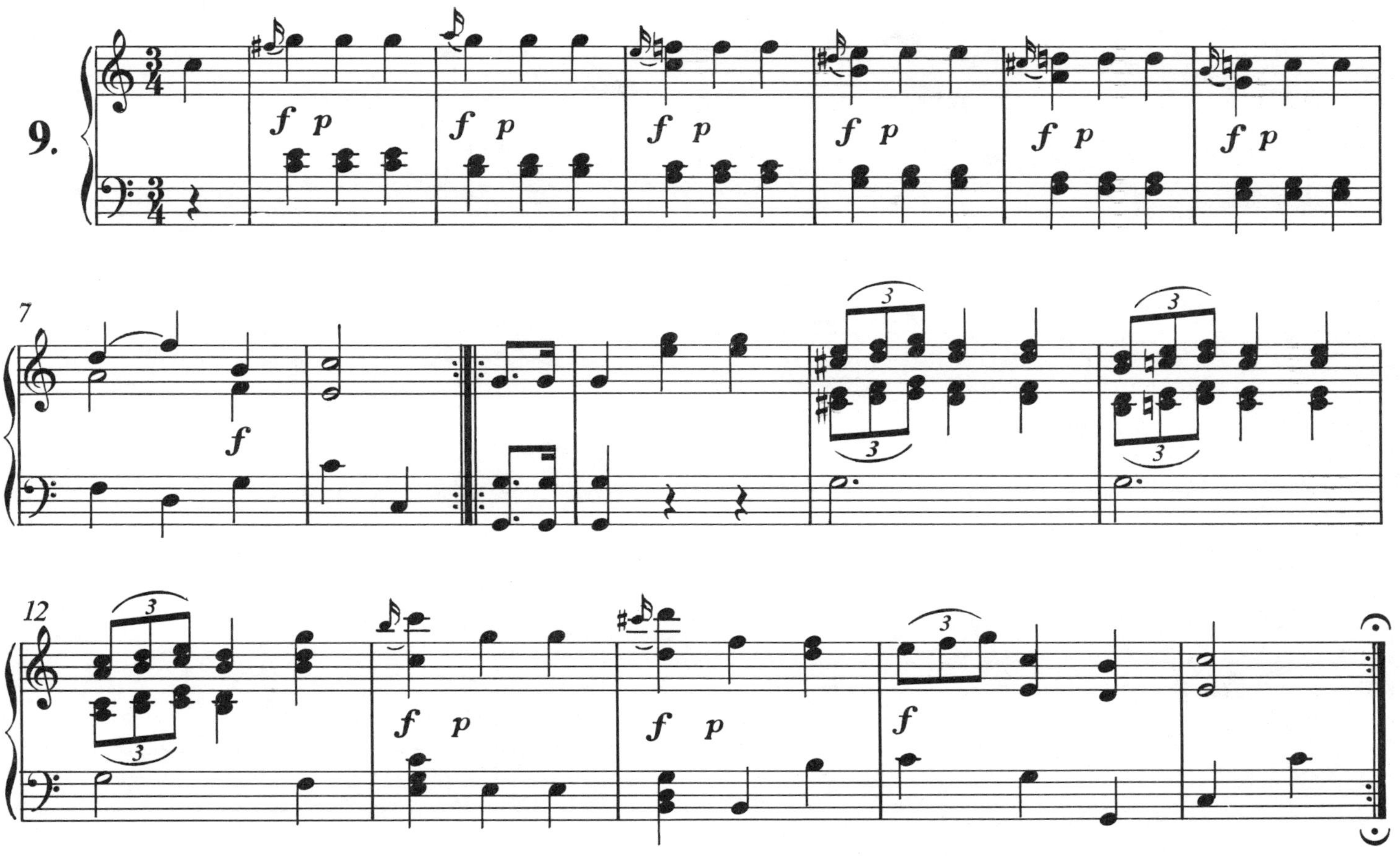

Trio

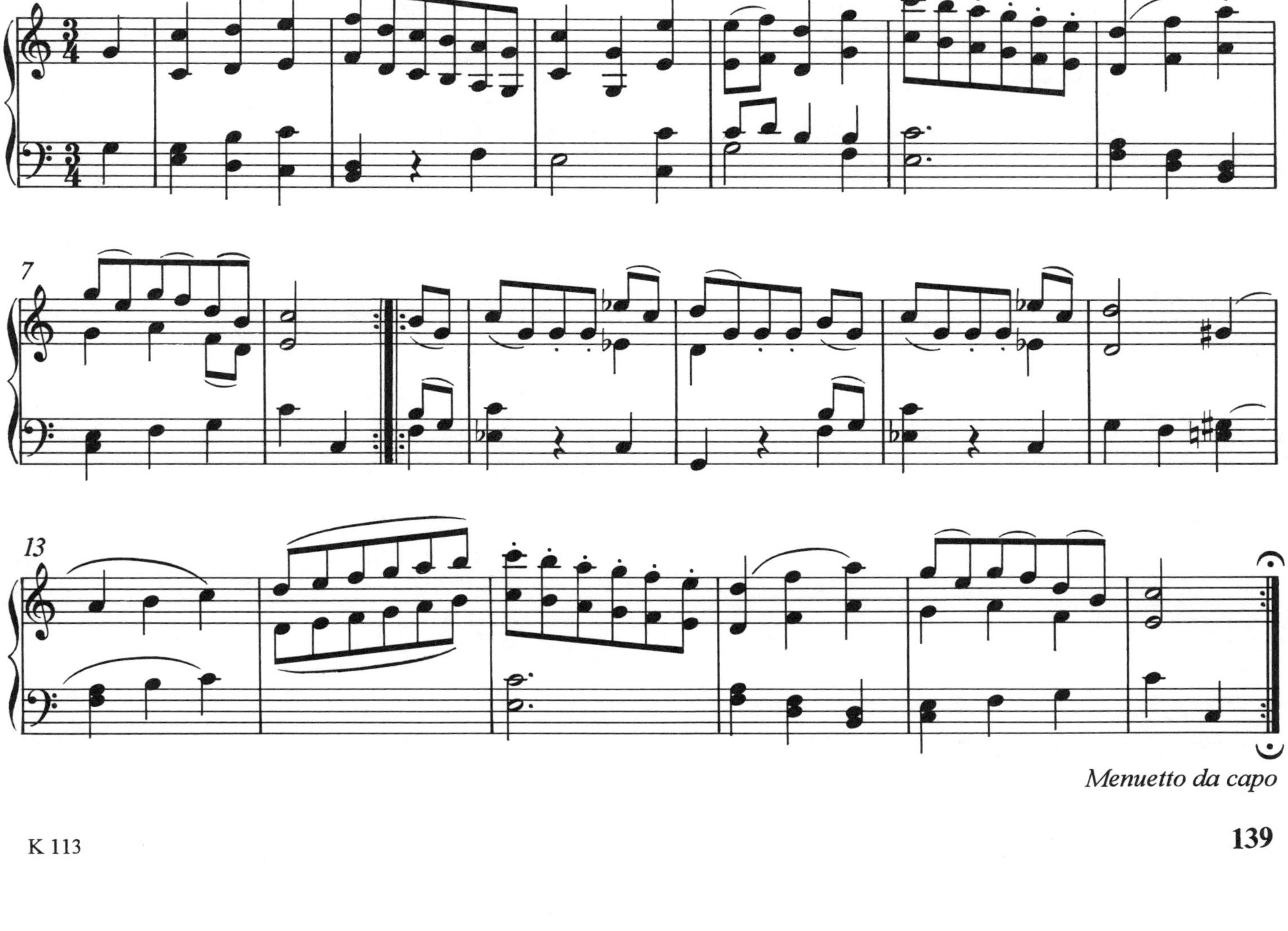

Menuetto da capo

10.

Trio

Menuetto da capo

11.

Trio

Menuetto da capo

Kontretänze

für Johann Rudolf Graf Czernin

KV 269ᵇ
Salzburg, ca 1777

2.

Andantino

p

staccato

5

tr

Allegro

p

f

15

p

f

21

p

27

f

3.

[Fine]

[da capo]

4.

8 Menuette

KV 315ª (315ᵍ)
Salzburg, ca 1773

1.

Trio

Menuetto da capo

K 113

2.

Trio

Menuetto da capo

3.

Trio

Menuetto da capo

K 113

4.

Trio

Menuetto da capo

5.

Trio

Menuetto da capo

6.

Trio

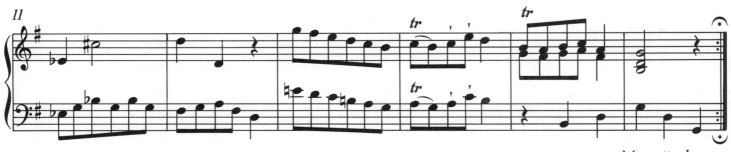

Menuetto da capo

7.

Trio

Menuetto da capo

8.

[Trio]

[Menuetto da capo]

K 113   Finis coronat opus   **153**

Marcia

KV 408/I (383°)
Wien, ca 1782

K 113

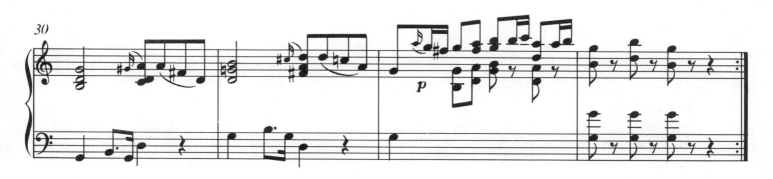

6 Tedeschi

No. 1

KV 509
Praga, 1787

Alternativo

Da capo

No. 2

Alternativo

Da capo

No. 3

Alternativo

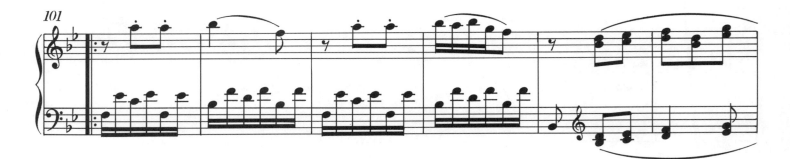

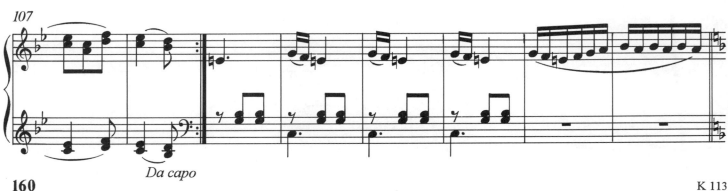

Da capo

No. 4

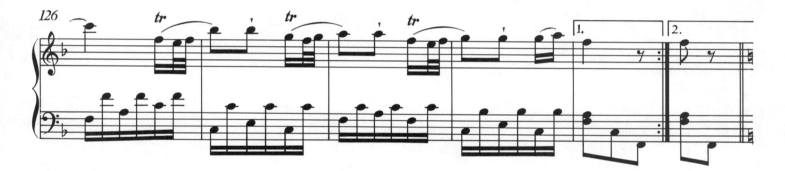

Alternativo

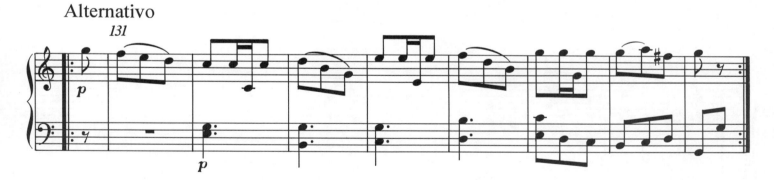

Da capo

No. 5

Alternativo

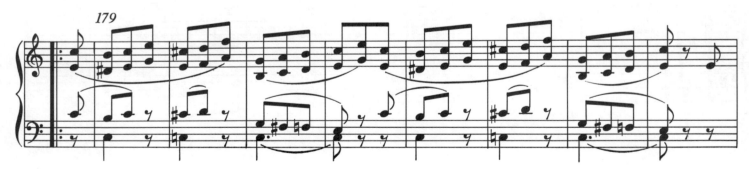

Da capo

No. 6

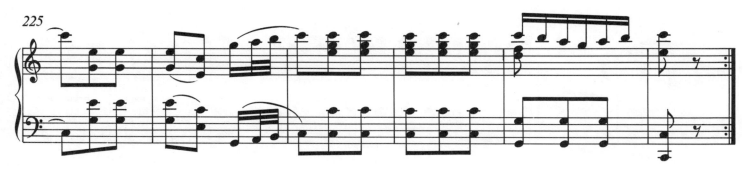

Alternativo

Da capo

Coda

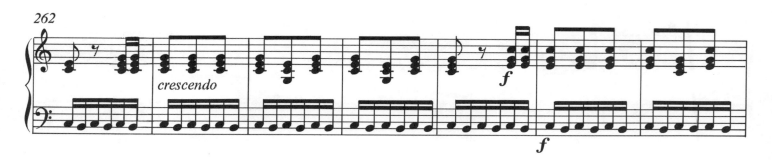

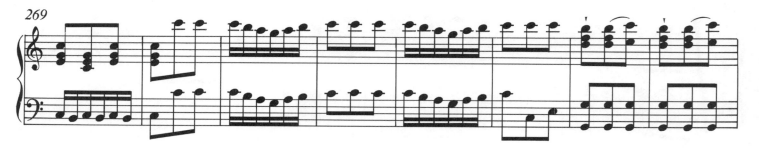

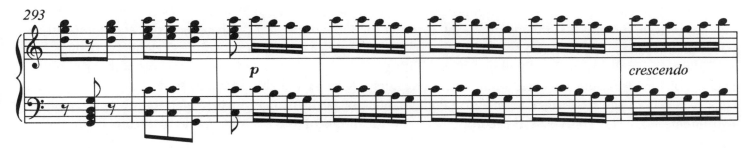

Notes

The present volume contains various individual piano works by Mozart. They are grouped as follows: (1) works of his childhood from Nannerl's notebook, (2) works of his childhood from the London sketchbook, (3) separate piano works, (4) the piano versions of orchestral dances and of a march.

(1) Nannerl's notebook. This notebook was given to Maria Anna (Nannerl) Mozart by her father as a present in 1759. Mozart's father entered the first works of Wolfgang into this notebook, which was later continued by Wolfgang himself. In the present volume seventeen authentic pieces have been included. In the course of editing the following sources were consulted: Nannerl's notebook, in the possession of the Mozarteum, Salzburg; the music to *Biographie W. A. Mozarts* by G. N. v. Nissen (Leipzig, Breitkopf & Härtel, 1828); and the sonatas for piano with violin accompaniment published as op. 1 (Paris: 1764) which represent a revised form of the piano versions of K 6, 7 and 8 included in this volume.

(2) Wolfgang entered music in the London sketchbook from 1764 onwards. Some are finished compositions (e.g. Nos. 1, 36, 37), others prove to be sketchy in character, their harmony, rhythm and part-writing being not elaborated (e.g. Nos. 7, 18, 32) and even notated with errors (e.g. Nos. 13, 20). In the case of certain items it emerges unambiguously that they were meant as drafts for some orchestral or chamber work and not as piano pieces (e.g. Nos. 15, 19, 35). The present edition publishes therefore the contents of the sketchbook (except for the fragments) unaltered and without comment. Only a few accidentals are added in brackets and some minor emendations made which are listed in the notes separately. Mozart probably intended to develop the sketches. Thus it is left to the performer to imagine their manner of performance, further elaboration and eventual instrumentation. The source of the edition was the facsimile of the sketchbook held in the Bibliotheka Jagellónska, Cracow.

(3) The sources of the separate piano works are the autograph manuscripts as well as the first and early editions and contemporary manuscript copies. (As regards autograph manuscripts only those of the nine piano pieces, K Anh. C 27.06 and of the Minuet in D major, K 355 (576^b) do not survive.)

(4) The piano versions of the orchestral dances and of the march cannot be considered genuine piano pieces. Some of them must have been the preliminary, compressed score-like notations of orchestral works, the rest are piano reductions made subsequently. In some cases Mozart's authorship is dubious, in other instances it cannot be safely established whether the piano reduction was made by Mozart or not. More detailed information on this topic can be found in the individual notes. Nevertheless, all surviving piano versions are included here, justified by the beauty of the works and their being relatively unknown. The sources were the autograph manuscripts, and contemporary copies and first editions, including the versions for piano and orchestra alike. The original titles of the works are printed in larger type, the titles in current use appear in small type.

Nannerl's Notebook

The movements of the sonata in C major for violin and piano, K 6 are as follows: *Allegro* (item No. 11 of the present edition), *Andante* (No. 12), Minuet I and Minuet II (Nos. 13 and 14) and a final *Allegro molto* whose piano version does not survive. Emendations made on the basis of the violin-piano version include:
K 6/I, bar 44, lower staff, the second half of the bar;
K 6/II, bar 9, lower staff, the first half of the bar; bar 33, lower staff, 3rd note;
K 6/IIIa–IIIb, the joining of the two Minuets to make a *da capo* form. The original articulation marks have been supplemented by signs printed in the violin–piano version.

Minuet, K 7/III, piece No. 15 in this edition.
In the violin–piano version it appears as Minuet I, the third movement of the sonata. Some articulation marks have been taken over from the printed version.

K 8/I, No. 16 of the present edition.
In the violin–piano version this is the opening movement of the sonata. The emendations made in this edition are based on this. These are: bar 5, lower staff, 13th note; bars 23-26 and 63-66, lower staff, ties; bar 33, lower staff, 13th note; bar 41, upper staff, the 1st appoggiatura. Some articulation marks have been taken from the printed version in this instance as well.

The London Sketchbook

K 15ᶜ (No. 3)
Bar 7, upper staff, the 4th note in the source is: b^1.

K 15ᵉ (No. 5)
Bars 13 and 14, lower staff, the 3rd and 4th notes in the source are: G, A.

K 15ᵗ (No. 19)
Bar 73, the upper staff is illegible in the source; another possible interpretation reads:

K 15ᵘ (No. 20)
The rhythm formula [♪. ♪ ♪] written thus by Mozart throughout is an obvious mistake. In the present edition it appears in the form of [♪. ♪♪] .

Separate Piano Works

Präludium in C, K 284ᵃ (300ᵍ)
Bar 17, upper staff, 4th beat: in the manuscript the note d^1 of the middle part runs into the trill sign written under the note f^1. In modern editions only the note f^1 can be found.

Ouverture (Suite) K 399 (385ⁱ)
The inscription "dans le Style de G. F. Händel", the tempo marking of the movements, some slurs, ties and dynamic marks are taken from the first edition of the work (Breitkopf, 1799).
Ouverture, bar 12, upper staff, 2nd beat: without c^2 in the autograph manuscript.
Courante, bars 18 and 44, lower staff: the slur above the five quavers can be interpreted as a tie for the bass notes in bars 18-19 and 44-45.

Adagio in B minor, K 540
On the basis of an early edition (Paris: Vogt & Veuve, c1797) the following signs have been added: bar 10, lower part, 3rd and 4th beats, tie; bar 36, upper part, slurs; bar 51ᵇ, 2nd half (i.e. secondo), slurs; from bar 51ᵇ onwards all dynamic marks.
Bar 55, upper staff, middle part, 3rd beat: in some modern editions *f sharp¹* is given here. Bar 57, upper staff, middle part, 1st beat: some modern editions contain b^1. In the sources none of these notes are found.

Piano Versions (Dances & March)

In the case of the piano versions of the orchestral dances and the march both the orchestral and the piano versions have been considered as authentic. For this reason some dynamic and phrase marks as well as staccato signs are taken over from the versions for orchestra. On the other hand, signs which contradict those included in the piano version as well as those referring to bowing rather than to phrasing have been left out of consideration.

12 Menuette K 103 (61ᵈ). This set of dances is most probably by M. Haydn and not by Mozart. The piano score however is by Mozart.

No. 2, Trio, bar 4, the upper staff in the piano version:
No. 8, Trio, bar 15,
the 1st beat is emended from an early Salzburg copy. In the other sources it reads:

Menuet in C, K 61ᵍ/II
It is questionable whether this work can be attributed to Mozart. The piano writing is, however, Mozart's. Orchestral version survives only of the Trio.

Menuet in D, K 94 (73ʰ)
The piano writing, which is evidently the compressed score-like notation of an orchestral score (see bars 10-12 and 21), originates from Mozart but the orchestral version does not survive.

11 Menuette, K 176
Only some sections of the piano writing are definitely by Mozart. The autograph manuscript of the orchestral version survives, however.

Kontretänze, K 269ᵇ
It is not sure that the piano writing originates from Mozart. Authentic orchestral versions survive in the case of Nos. 2 and 4. No. 3 is possibly incomplete. The editor's suggestion (*da capo–Fine*) is intended as an aid to performance.

8 Menuette, K 315ᵃ (315ᵍ)
The piano score survives both in Mozart's autograph manuscript and in a contemporary copy; no orchestral version is known. It is disputed whether the trio of No. 8 belongs here.

Marcia in C, K 408/1 (383ᵉ)
Both the piano score and the orchestral instrumentation originate from Mozart.

6 Tedeschi, K 509
Mozart's remark for the performance of the orchestral version reads as follows: "Jeder Teutsche hat sein Trio, oder vielmehr Alternativo; – nach dem Alternativo wird der Teutsche widerhollet, dann wieder das alternativo; dann geht es durch den Eingang weiter in den folgenden Teutschen." (Each Tedesca has its trio or rather its alternativo; – after the alternativo the Tedesca is repeated, then the alternativo again; thereafter it continues through the transition to the following Tedesca.)
In the piano version the inscription "Minore" instead of "Alternativo" is found.

© 1994 for this edition by Könemann Music Budapest Kft.
H-1137 Budapest, Szent István park 3.

K 113/2

Distributed worldwide by
Könemann Verlagsgesellschaft mbH, Bonner Str. 126.
D-50968 Köln

Responsible co-editor: Tamás Zászkaliczky
Production: Detlev Schaper
Cover design: Peter Feierabend
Technical editor: Dezső Varga
Engraved by Kottamester Bt., Budapest:
Balázs Bata, János Bihari, Zsuzsanna Czúni, Mrs. Erzsébet Malaczkó,
Márta Kercza

Printed by Kossuth Printing House Co., Budapest
Printed in Hungary

ISBN 963 8303 26 3